Overview

"i C#" is an essential resource designed to help both entry-level and experienced programmers prepare for C# (C Sharp) programming interviews with confidence. Whether you're a recent graduate or a seasoned developer looking to switch jobs or advance your career, this book offers a well-organized collection of interview questions and in-depth answers that cover a wide range of C# topics.

Key Features:

- *Extensive Question Coverage: This guide covers a broad spectrum of C# topics, including language fundamentals, object-oriented programming, multithreading, asynchronous programming, LINQ, error handling, and more.*

- *Clear Explanations: Each question is accompanied by a detailed explanation that not only provides the correct answer but also delves into the reasoning behind it.*

- *Real-World Scenarios: The book presents questions with answers from real-world scenarios and challenges.*

- *Advanced Topics: For those aiming to demonstrate expertise, the book includes advanced questions on topics like memory management, performance optimization, design patterns, and more.*

With its comprehensive coverage and detailed explanations, this book serves as both a study guide and a reference for anyone looking to master the intricacies of C# programming and succeed in interviews.

C# Interview Question:

1. What is C#

C# (pronounced "See Sharp") is a modern, object-oriented, and type-safe programming language. C# enables developers to build many types of secure and robust applications that run in .NET. C# is an ***object-oriented, component-oriented*** programming language. C# provides language constructs to directly support these concepts, making C# a natural language in which to create and use software components. Since its origin, C# has added features to support new workloads and emerging software design practices. At its core, C# is an object-oriented language. Its syntax is similar to C++ syntax and meets 100% of the requirements of OOPs like the following:

- Abstraction
- Encapsulation
- Polymorphism
- Inheritance

2. What is an Object?

According to MSDN, "*a class or struct definition is like a blueprint that specifies what the type can do. An object is basically a block of memory that has been allocated and configured according to the blueprint. A program may create many objects of the same class. Objects are also called instances, and they can be stored in either a named variable or in an array or collection. Client code is the code that uses these variables to call the methods and access the public properties of the object. In an object-oriented language such as C#, a typical program consists of multiple objects interacting dynamically*".

Objects helps us to access the member of a class or struct either they can be fields, methods or properties, by using the dot.

Confused? Well, Don't be confused. See the below examples of real-world entities.

Seeing this image, you will say, "This is a laptop". Right? What about this?

You'll say it's a Pen.

Actually, the first image is not a laptop and the second image is not of a pen. Then what is that?

Well, the first image is a type of laptop and the second one is a type of pen.

According to OOPS, a class is a blueprint used to generate a collection of homogenous products, referred to as objects.

Consider you are using a laptop of company XYZ, that is an object of Laptop Class.

There are two things that all real-world objects have in common: state and behaviour.

Laptops have states (name, colour, processors) and behaviour (ON, OFF, Audio, Video).

A great way to start thinking about object-oriented programming is to identify the state and behaviour of real-world objects.

Objects in OOPs are conceptually identical to real-world objects. From a Technical point of view, An entity with a clearly defined structure and behaviour is called an object. An object in OOPs can include:

- A Variable.
- A Data Structure.
- A Function or

- A   method.

When an object is instantiated, heap memory is allocated at runtime.

3. What is Managed or Unmanaged Code?

Managed   **Code**

"The code, which is developed in .NET framework is known as managed code. This code is directly executed by CLR with the help of managed code execution. Any language that is written in .NET Framework is managed code". OR

"The resource, which is with in your application domain is, managed code. The resources that are within domain are faster. Managed code uses CLR which in turns looks after your applications by managing memory, handling security, allowing cross - language debugging, and so on".

Unmanaged   **Code**

The code, which is developed outside .NET framework is known   as   unmanaged   code.

"Applications that do not run under the control of the CLR are said to be unmanaged, and certain languages such as C++ can be used to write such applications, which, for example, access low - level functions of the operating system. Background compatibility with the code of VB, ASP and COM are examples of unmanaged code".

Unmanaged code can be unmanaged source code and unmanaged compile code. Unmanaged code is executed with   the   help   of   wrapper   classes.

Wrapper classes are of two types:

- CCW (COM Callable Wrapper).

- RCW (Runtime Callable Wrapper).

1   4. What is Boxing and Unboxing?

Answer: Boxing and Unboxing both are used for type conversion but have some difference:

Boxing:

Boxing is the process of converting a value type data type to the object or to any interface data type which is implemented by this value type. When the CLR boxes a value means when CLR is converting a value type to Object Type, it wraps the value inside a System.Object and stores it on the heap area in application domain.

Example:

```
public void Function1()
{
    int i = 111;
    object o = i;//implicit Boxing
    Console.WriteLine(o);
}
```

Boxing is used to store value types in the garbage-collected heap. Boxing is an implicit conversion of a *value* type to the type *object* or to any interface type implemented by this value type. Boxing a value type allocates an object instance on the heap and copies the value into the new object.

Unboxing:

Unboxing is also a process which is used to extract the value type from the object or any implemented interface type. Boxing may be done implicitly, but unboxing have to be explicit by code.

Example:

```
public void Function1()
{
    object o = 111;
    int i = (int)o;//explicit Unboxing
    Console.WriteLine(i);
}
```

For the unboxing of value types to succeed at run time, the item being unboxed must be a reference to an object that was previously created by boxing an instance of that value type.

The concept of boxing and unboxing underlines the C# unified view of the type system in which a value of any type can be treated as an object.

5. What is the difference between a struct and a class in C#?

Answer:

Class and struct both are the user defined data type but have some major difference:

Struct

- The struct is value type in C# and it inherits from System.Value Type.
- Struct is usually used for smaller amounts of data.
- Struct can't be inherited to other type.
- A structure can't be abstract.

- No need to create object by new keyword.
- Do not have permission to create any default constructor.

Class

- The class is reference type in C# and it inherits from the System.Object Type.
- Classes are usually used for large amounts of data.
- Classes can be inherited to other class.
- A class can be abstract type.
- We can't use an object of a class with using new keyword.
- We can create a default constructor.

In this way, struct should be used only when you are sure that,

- It logically represents a single value, like primitive types (int, double, etc.).
- It is immutable.
- It should not be boxed and un-boxed frequently.

In all other cases, you should define your types as classes.

6. What is the difference between Interface and Abstract Class?

Answer:

The key differences between abstract classes and interfaces are as follows:

- Abstract classes can contain implemented methods, while interfaces only contain method signatures.

- Classes can implement multiple interfaces, but they can inherit from only one abstract class.
- Abstract classes can have constructors, while interfaces cannot.
- Abstract classes can have fields and properties, while interfaces can only have properties.
- Abstract classes are typically used for creating a base class for other classes to inherit from, while interfaces are used for defining a contract that classes must implement.

When to Use an Abstract Class vs When to Use an Interface in C#

As a general rule, you should use an abstract class when creating a base class that needs to be inherited by other classes in a class hierarchy. If you need to define a behavior that can be implemented by multiple unrelated classes, you should use an interface.

If you need to add new members or behavior to a base class, you can add them to an abstract class. However, if you need to add behavior to an existing class that cannot inherit from a new base class, you can use an interface.

Another important consideration when deciding between an abstract class and an interface is the level of abstraction needed. Abstract classes can provide a higher level of abstraction than interfaces, as they can include both abstract and non-abstract members. Interfaces, on the other hand, only include abstract members.

It's also worth noting that while a class can inherit from multiple interfaces, it can only inherit from one abstract class. This means that if you need to provide multiple behaviors to a class, using interfaces may be a better option.

Advantages of Using Abstract Classes Over Interfaces in Certain Scenarios

When creating a hierarchy of classes, abstract classes can provide a more structured approach than interfaces.

They allow for the creation of a more hierarchical class structure and can provide a base implementation for derived classes to reuse.
If you need to provide a common implementation for a group of derived classes, you can use an abstract class. This can help reduce code duplication and improve maintainability.

Advantages of Using Interfaces Over Abstract Classes in Certain Scenarios

Interfaces can provide a more flexible approach than abstract classes for defining a contract. They provide a way to define behavior that can be implemented by multiple unrelated classes without requiring inheritance. This makes interfaces a better choice when you need to define behavior that can be implemented by classes that don't share a common ancestor.

7. What is enum in C#?

Answer:

An enum is a value type with a set of related named constants often referred to as an enumerator list. The enum keyword is used to declare an enumeration. It is a primitive data type, which is user defined.

An enum type can be an integer (float, int, byte, double etc.). But if you used beside int it has to be cast.

An enum is used to create numeric constants in .NET framework. All the members of enum are of enum type. Their must be a numeric value for each enum type.

The default underlying type of the enumeration element is int. By default, the first enumerator has the value 0, and the value of each successive enumerator is increased by

```
1.  enum Dow {Sat, Sun, Mon, Tue, Wed, Thu, Fri};
```

Some points about enum

- Enums are enumerated data type in c#.
- Enums are not for end-user, they are meant for developers.
- Enums are strongly typed constant. They are strongly typed, i.e. an enum of one type may not be implicitly assigned to an enum of another type even though the underlying value of their members are the same.
- Enumerations (enums) make your code much more readable and understandable.
- Enum values are fixed. Enum can be displayed as a string and processed as an integer.
- The default type is int, and the approved types are byte, sbyte, short, ushort, uint, long, and ulong.
- Every enum type automatically derives from System.Enum and thus we can use System.Enum methods on enums.
- Enums are value types and are created on the stack and not on the heap.

8. What is the difference between "continue" and "break" statements in C#?

Answer:

Using break statement, you can 'jump out of a loop' whereas by using continue statement, you can 'jump over one iteration' and then resume your loop execution.

Eg. Break Statement

```
1. using System;
```

```
2.   using System.Collections;
3.   using System.Linq;
4.   using System.Text;
5.
6.   namespace break_example
7.       {
8.           Class brk_stmt {
9.               public static void main(String[]
     args) {
10.                     for (int i = 0; i <= 5; i++)
     {
11.                         if (i == 4) {
12.                             break;
13.                         }
14.                         Console.WriteLine("The nu
     mber is " + i);
15.                         Console.ReadLine();
16.
17.                     }
18.                 }
19.             }
20.
21.         }
```

Output

The number is 0;
The number is 1;
The number is 2;
The number is 3;

Eg.Continue Statement

```
1.   using System;
2.   using System.Collections;
3.   using System.Linq;
4.   using System.Text;
5.
6.   namespace continue_example
7.   {
8.       Class cntnu_stmt
9.       {
10.          public static void main(String[]
11.          {
12.              for (int i = 0; i <= 5; i++)
13.              {
14.                  if (i == 4)
```

```
15.                      {
16.                          continue;
17.                      }
18.                      Console.WriteLine("The number
    is "+ i);
19.                      Console.ReadLine();
20.
21.                  }
22.              }
23.          }
24.
25. }
26.
27.
```

OutputThe number is 1;
The number is 2;
The number is 3;
The number is 5;

9. What is the difference between constant and read only in c#?

Answer:

Constant (const) and **Readonly** (readonly) both looks like same as per the uses but they have some differences:

Constant is known as "const" keyword in C# which is also known immutable values which are known at compile time and do not change their values at run time like in any function or constructor for the life of application till the application is running.

Readonly is known as "readonly" keyword in C# which is also known immutable values and are known at compile and run time and do not change their values at run time like in any function for the life of application till the application is running. You can assay their value by constructor when we call constructor with "new" keyword.

See **the** **example**

We have a Test Class in which we have two variables one is readonly and another is constant.

```
1.  class Test {
2.      readonly int read = 10;
3.      const int cons = 10;
4.      public Test() {
5.          read = 100;
6.          cons = 100;
7.      }
8.      public void Check() {
9.          Console.WriteLine("Read only : {0}",
    read);
10.         Console.WriteLine("const : {0}", cons
    );
11.     }
12. }
```

Here I was trying to change the value of both the variables in constructor but when I am trying to change the constant it gives an error to change their value in that block which have to call at run time.

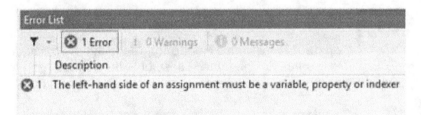

So finally remove that line of code from class and call this Check() function like the following code snippet:

```
1.  class Program {
2.      static void Main(string[] args) {
3.          Test obj = new Test();
4.          obj.Check();
5.          Console.ReadLine();
6.      }
7.  }
8.  class Test {
9.      readonly int read = 10;
10.     const int cons = 10;
```

```
11.     public Test() {
12.          read = 100;
13.     }
14.     public void Check() {
15.          Console.WriteLine("Read only : {0}",
    read);
16.          Console.WriteLine("const : {0}", cons
    );
17.     }
18. }
```

Output:

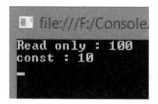

10. What is the difference between ref and out keywords?

Answer:

In C Sharp (C#) we can have three types of parameters in a function. The parameters can be in parameter (which is not returned back to the caller of the function), out parameter and ref parameter. We have lots of differences in   both   of   them.

Ref	Out
The parameter or argument must be initialized first before it is passed to ref.	It is not compulsory to initialize a parameter or argument before it is passed to an out.
It is not required to assign or initialize the value of a parameter (which is passed by ref) before returning to the calling method.	A called method is required to assign or initialize a value of a parameter (which is passed to an out) before returning to the calling method.
Passing a parameter value by Ref is useful when the called method is also needed to modify the pass parameter.	Declaring a parameter to an out method is useful when multiple values need to be returned from a function or method.
It is not compulsory to initialize a parameter value before using it in a calling method.	A parameter value must be initialized within the calling method before its use.
When we use REF, data can be passed bi-directionally.	When we use OUT data is passed only in a unidirectional way (from the called method to the caller method).

Both ref and out are treated differently at run time and they are treated the same at compile time.

Properties are not variables, therefore it cannot be passed as an out or ref parameter.

11. Can "this" be used within a static method?

Answer:

We can't use this in static method because keyword 'this' returns a reference to the current instance of the class containing it. Static methods (or any static member) do not belong to a particular instance. They exist without creating an instance of the class and call with the name of a class not by instance so we can't use this keyword in the body of static Methods, but in case of Extension Methods we can use it the functions parameters. Let's have a look on "this" keyword.

The "this" keyword is a special type of reference variable that is implicitly defined within each constructor and non-static method as a first parameter of the type class in which it is defined. For example, consider the following class written in C#.

12. Define Property in C#.net?

Answer:

Properties are members that provide a flexible mechanism to read, write or compute the values of private fields, in other words by the property we can access private fields. In other words we can say that a property is a return type function/method with one parameter or without a parameter. These are always public data members. It uses methods to access and assign values to private fields called accessors.

Now question is what are accessors?

The get and set portions or blocks of a property are called accessors. These are useful to restrict the accessibility of a property, the set accessor specifies that we can assign a value to a private field in a property and without the set accessor property it is like a read-only field. By the get accessor we can access the value of the private field, in other words it returns a single value. A Get accessor specifies that we can access the value of a field publically.

We have the three types of properties

- Read/Write.
- ReadOnly.
- WriteOnly

Property Access Modifiers in C#

Access modifiers define the access level of a property, whether a property can be accessed by any caller program, within an assembly, or just within a class.
The following table describes access level modifiers.

- Public - Any other code can access the type or member in the same assembly or another assembly that references it.
- Private - The type or member can be accessed only by code in the same class or struct.

- Protected - The type or member can be accessed only by code in the same class or in a class that is derived from that class.
- Internal - The type or member can be accessed by any code in the same assembly but not from another assembly.
- Any code can access protected internal - The type or member in the assembly in which it is declared or from within a derived class in another assembly.
- Private protected - The type or member can be accessed only within its declaring assembly, by code in the same class, or in a type derived from that class.

13. What is extension method in c# and how to use them?

Answer:

Extension methods enable you to add methods to existing types without creating a new derived type, recompiling, or otherwise modifying the original type. An extension method is a special kind of static method, but they are called as if they were instance methods on the extended type.

How to use extension methods?

An extension method is a static method of a static class, where the "this" modifier is applied to the first parameter. The type of the first parameter will be the type that is extended.

Extension methods are only in scope when you explicitly import the namespace into your source code with a using directive.

Like: suppose we have a class like bellow:

```
1.  public class Class1 {
2.      public string Display() {
3.          return ("I m in Display");
4.      }
5.
6.      public string Print() {
7.          return ("I m in Print");
8.      }
9.  }
```

Now we need to extend the definition of this class so m going to create a static class to create an extinction method like:

```
1.  public static class XX {
2.      public static void NewMethod(this Class1
    ob) {
3.          Console.WriteLine("Hello I m extended
    method");
4.      }
5.  }
```

Here I just create a method that name is NewMethod with a parameter using this to define which type of data I need to be extend, now let's see how to use this function.

```
using System;
using System.Text;
using ClassLibExtMethod;

namespace ExtensionMethod1
{
    public static class XX
    {
        public static void NewMethod(this Class1 ob)
        {
            Console.WriteLine("Hello I m extended method");
        }
    }
    class Program
    {
        static void Main(string[] args)
        {
            Class1 ob = new Class1();
            ob.Display();
            ob.Print();
            ob.|
                                     y();
                Display
        }       Equals
                GetHashCode
    }           GetType
}               NewMethod        (extension) void Class1.NewMethod()
                Print
                ToString
```

```
1.  class Program {
2.      static void Main(string[] args) {
3.          Class1 ob = new Class1();
4.          ob.Display();
5.          ob.Print();
6.          ob.NewMethod();
7.          Console.ReadKey();
8.      }
9.  }
```

Output will be:

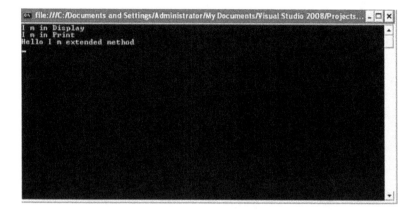

14. What is the difference between dispose and finalize methods in c#?

Answer: finalizer and dispose both are used for same task like to free unmanaged resources but have some differences   see.

Finalize:

- Finalize used to free unmanaged resources those are not in use like files, database connections in application domain and more, held by an object before that object is destroyed.
- In the Internal process it is called by Garbage Collector and can't called manual by user code or any service.
- Finalize belongs to System.Object class.
- Implement it when you have unmanaged resources in your code, and make sure that these resources are freed when the Garbage collection happens.

Dispose:

- Dispose is also used to free unmanaged resources those are not in use like files, database connections in Application domain at any time.
- Dispose explicitly it is called by manual user code.
- If we need to dispose method so must implement that class by IDisposable interface.
- It belongs to IDisposable interface.
- Implement this when you are writing a custom class that will be used by other users.

There are various key differences between Dispose() and Finalize() methods. Some of the key differences between Dispose() and Finalize() methods are as follows:

1. The dispose() method is described in the IDisposable interface. In contrast, the finalize() method is described in the class object.

2. After implementing the interface IDisposable, the method dispose() is implemented in a class. In contrast, the finalize() method must be implemented solely for unmanaged resources because the garbage collector automatically frees managed resources.

3. The dispose() method is frees and fast the object instantly, and thus it has no effect on performance. In contrast, the finalize() method is slower and doesn't immediately liberate the resources owned by the object.

4. A programmer must explicitly invoke the discard() method within the code. In contrast, the trash collector automatically invokes the finalize() method before destroying the object.

5. The dispose() method access's specifier is public since it is described in the interface IDisposable and would be executed by the class that implements this interface. Therefore it must be public. In contrast, the finalize() method includes a protected access specifier, which means it should not be accessible to any members outside the class.

6. The Dispose() method has no performance implications. In contrast, performance costs are associated with the Finalize() method because it does not automatically wipe the memory and is not invoked by the GC automatically.

7. The dispose() method can be called at any moment. In contrast, the garbage collector calls the finalize() method when it discovers that an object has not been referenced in a long time.

8. The discard() method has no effect on application speed. In contrast, the finalize() method may reduce program performance.

15. What is the difference between string and StringBuilder in c#?

Answer:

StringBuilder and string both use to store string value but both have many differences on the bases of instance creation and also for performance:

String:

String is an immutable object. Immutable like when we create string object in code so we cannot modify or change that object in any operations like insert new value, replace or append any value with existing value in string object, when we have to do some operations to change string simply it will dispose the old value of string object and it will create new instance in memory for hold the new value in string object like:

```
class Program
{
    static void Main(string[] args)
    {
        string val = "Hello";
        // create a new string instance instead of changing the old one
        val += "am ";
        val += "Nitin Pandit";
        Console.WriteLine(val);
    }
}
```

Note:

- It's an immutable object that hold string value.
- Performance wise string is slow because its' create a new instance to override or change the previous value.
- String belongs to System namespace.

StringBuilder:

System.Text.Stringbuilder is mutable object which also hold the string value, mutable means once we create a System.Text.Stringbuilder object we can use this object for any operation like insert value in existing string with insert functions also replace or append without creating new instance of System.Text.Stringbuilder for every time so it's use the previous object so it's work fast as compare than System.String. Let's have an example to understand   System.Text.Stringbuilder   like:

```
class Program
{
    static void Main(string[] args)
    {
        StringBuilder val = new StringBuilder("");
        val.Append("hello");
        val.Append(" am Nitin Pandit :)");
        Console.WriteLine(val);
    }
}
```
Note:

- StringBuilder is a mutable object.
- Performance wise StringBuilder is very fast because it will use same instance of StringBuilder object to perform any operation like insert value in existing string.
- StringBuilder belongs to System.Text.Stringbuilder namespace.

16. What is delegates in C# and uses of delegates?

Answer:

C# delegates are same as pointers to functions, in C or C++. A delegate Object is a reference type variable that use to holds the reference to a method. The reference can be changed at runtime which is hold by an object of delegate, a delegate object can hold many functions reference which is also known as Invocation List that refers functions in a sequence FIFO, we can new functions ref in this list at run time by += operator and can remove by -= operator.

A delegate is a type that represents references to methods with a particular parameter list and return type. When you instantiate a delegate, you can associate its instance with any method with a compatible signature and return type. You can invoke (or call) the method through the delegate instance.

Delegates are especially used for implementing events and the call-back methods. All delegates are implicitly derived from the System.Delegate class.

Let's see how to use Delegate with Example:

```
class Program
{
    static void Main(string[] args)
    {
        TestDelegate obj = new TestDelegate();
        obj.delObject("Nitin");
    }
}
delegate void Del(string UserName);
class TestDelegate
{
    public Del delObject;
    public TestDelegate()
    {
        delObject = new Del(this.SayHello);
    }
    public void SayHello(string UserName)
    {
        Console.WriteLine("Hello.." + UserName);
    }
}
```

Delegates have the following properties:
- Delegates are similar to C++ function pointers, but delegates are fully object-oriented, and unlike C++ pointers to member functions, delegates encapsulate both an object instance and a method.
- Delegates allow methods to be passed as parameters.
- Delegates can be used to define callback methods.
- Delegates can be chained together; for example, multiple methods can be called on a single event.
- Methods don't have to match the delegate type exactly. Lambda expressions are a more concise way of writing inline code blocks. Lambda expressions (in certain contexts) are compiled to delegate types.

17. What is sealed class in c#?

Answer:

Sealed classes are used to restrict the inheritance feature of object oriented programming. Once a class is defined as a sealed class, the class cannot be inherited.

In C#, the sealed modifier is used to define a class as sealed. In Visual Basic .NET the Not Inheritable keyword serves the purpose of sealed. If a class is derived from a sealed class then the compiler throws an error.

If you have ever noticed, structs are sealed. You cannot derive a class from a struct.

The following class definition defines a sealed class in C#:

```
1.  // Sealed class
2.  sealed class SealedClass
3.  {
4.
5.  }
```

Unlike a struct, which is implicitly sealed, a sealed class is declared with the keyword, "sealed" to prevent accidental inheritance of the class. A sealed class can be useful only if it has methods with public-level accessibility. A sealed class cannot be an abstract class as the abstract class is intended to be derived by another class that provides implementation for the abstract methods and properties.

For example, a sealed class, DatabaseHelper, can be designed with properties and methods that can service the functionalities of database-related actions, including open- and closed-database connection, fetch and update data, etc. Because it performs crucial functions that should not be tampered with by overriding in its derived classes, it can be designed as sealed class.

Sealing restricts the benefit of extensibility and prevents customization of library types. Hence, a class has to be sealed after carefully weighing the impact of sealing it. The list of criteria to consider for sealing a class includes:

- The class is static
- The class contains inherited members that represent sensitive information
- The class is queried to retrieve its attributes through the reflection method
- The class inherits many virtual members that need to be sealed

18. What are partial classes?

Answer:

A partial class is only use to splits the definition of a class in two or more classes in a same source code file or more than one source files. You can create a class definition in multiple files but it will be compiled as one class at run time and also when you'll create an instance of this class so you can access all the methods from all source file with a same object.

Partial Classes can be create in the same namespace it's doesn't allowed to create a partial class in different namespace. So use "partial" keyword with all the class name which you want to bind together with the same name of class in same namespace, let's have an example:

```csharp
partial class Class1
{
    public void Function1()
    {
        Console.WriteLine("Function 1 ");
    }
}
partial class Class1
{
    public void Function2()
    {
        Console.WriteLine("Function 2 ");
    }
}
class Program
{
    static void Main(string[] args)
    {
        Class1 obj = new Class1();
        obj.Function1();
        obj.Function2();
        Console.ReadLine();
    }
}
```

19. What is IEnumerable<> in c#?

Answer:

IEnumerable is the parent interface for all non-generic collections in System.Collections namespace like ArrayList, HastTable etc. that can be enumerated. For the generic version of this interface as IEnumerable<T> which a parent interface of all generic collections class in System.Collections.Generic namespace like List<> and more.

In System.Collections.Generic.IEnumerable<T> have only a single method which is GetEnumerator() that returns an IEnumerator. IEnumerator provides the power to iterate through the collection by exposing a Current property and Move Next and Reset methods, if we doesn't have this interface as a parent so we can't use iteration by foreach loop or can't use that class object in our LINQ query.

```
*○ System.Collections.Generic.IEnumerable< out T>                                        ▾
  ⊞ Assembly mscorlib.dll, v4.0.0.0

    using System.Collections;

  ⊟namespace System.Collections.Generic
   {
  ⊟    // Summary:
       //     Exposes the enumerator, which supports a simple iteration over a collection
       //     of a specified type.To browse the .NET Framework source code for this type,
       //     see the Reference Source.
       //
       // Type parameters:
       //   T:
       //     The type of objects to enumerate.This type parameter is covariant. That is,
       //     you can use either the type you specified or any type that is more derived.
       //     For more information about covariance and contravariance, see Covariance
       //     and Contravariance in Generics.
  ⊟    public interface IEnumerable<out T> : IEnumerable
       {
  ⊟        // Summary:
         //     Returns an enumerator that iterates through the collection.
         //
         // Returns:
         //     An enumerator that can be used to iterate through the collection.
         IEnumerator<T> GetEnumerator();
       }
   }
```

20. What is difference between late binding and early binding in c#?

Answer:

Early Binding and Late Binding concepts belongs to polymorphism so let's see first about polymorphism:

Polymorphism is an ability to take more than one form of a function means with a same name we can write multiple functions code in a same class or any derived class.

Polymorphism we have 2 different types to achieve that:

- Compile Time also known as Early Binding or Overloading.
- Run Time also known as Late Binding or Overriding.

Compile Time Polymorphism or Early Binding:

In Compile time polymorphism or Early Binding we will use multiple methods with same name but different type of parameter or may be the number or parameter because of this we can perform different-different tasks with same method name in the same class which is also known as Method overloading.

See how we can do that by the following example:

```csharp
class MyMath
{
    public int Sum(int val1, int val2)
    {
        return val1 + val2;
    }
    public string Sum(string val1, string val2)
    {
        return val1 + " " + val2;
    }
}
```

Run Time Polymorphism or Late Binding:

Run time polymorphism also known as late binding, in Run Time polymorphism or Late Binding we can do use same method names with same signatures means same type or same number of parameters but not in same class because compiler doesn't allowed that at compile time so we can use in derived class that bind at run time when a child class or derived class object will instantiated that's way we says that Late Binding. For that we have to create my parent class functions as partial and in driver or child class as override functions with override keyword.

Likeas following example:

```csharp
class Class1
{
    public virtual string TestFunction()
    {
        return "Hello";
    }
}
class Class2 : Class1
{
    public override string TestFunction()
    {
        return "Bye Bye";
    }
}
class Program
{
    static void Main(string[] args)
    {
        Class2 obj = new Class2();
        Console.WriteLine(obj.TestFunction());
        Console.ReadLine();
    }
}
```

Use Early Binding When:

- Performance Matters: Early binding offers better performance since method resolution is known at compile-time, resulting in faster execution.

- Compile-Time Safety: Early binding is the preferred choice when you want to catch errors during compilation time. It helps in detecting issues before runtime.
- Known Types and Fixed Behavior: Early binding is suitable when you know the types and behavior of objects at compile-time, and they won't change during program execution.
- Static and Predictable Scenarios: Early binding is a more appropriate option for scenarios where the method or object references are static and known at compile time.

Use Late Binding When:

- Dynamic Behavior Needed: When you require dynamic behavior, where specific implementations are determined at runtime based on conditions or external factors.
- Uncertain Types at Compile-Time: Late binding is useful when dealing with objects or types whose specifics are uncertain during compilation, such as when working with external components, plugins, or COM objects.
- Interoperability with External Components: Late binding is often used when interacting with external libraries or components with unknown types, as it enables the code to work with varying types at runtime.

21. What are the differences between IEnumerable and IQueryable?

Answer:

Before the differences learn what is IEnumerable and IQueryable.

IEnumerable:

Is the parent interface for all non-generic collections in System.Collections namespace like ArrayList, HastTable etc. that can be enumerated. For the generic version of this interface as IEnumerable<T> which a parent interface of all generic collections class in System.Collections.Generic namespace like List<> and more.

IQueryable:

As per MSDN IQueryable interface is intended for implementation by query providers. It is only supposed to be implemented by providers that also implement IQueryable<T>. If the provider does not also implement IQueryable<T>, the standard query operators cannot be used on the provider's data source.

The IQueryable interface inherits the IEnumerable interface so that if it represents a query, the results of that query can be enumerated. Enumeration causes the expression tree associated with an IQueryable object to be executed. The definition of "executing an expression tree" is specific to a query provider. For example, it may involve translating the expression tree to an appropriate query language for the underlying data source. Queries that do not return enumerable results are executed when the Execute method is called.

IEnumerable	IQueryable
IEnumerable belongs to System.Collections namespace.	IQueryable belongs to System.Linq namespace.
IEnumerable is the best way to write query on collections data type like List, Array etc.	IQueryable is the best way to write query data like remote database, service collections.
IEnumerable is the return type for LINQ to Object and LINQ to XML queries.	IQueryable is the return type of LINQ to SQL queries.
IEnumerable doesn't support lazy loading. So it's not a recommended approach for paging kind of scenarios.	IQueryable support lazy loading so we can also use in paging kind of scenarios.
Extension methods are supports by IEnumerable takes functional objects for LINQ Query's.	IQueryable implements IEnumerable so indirectly it's also supports Extensions methods.

22. What happens if the inherited interfaces have conflicting method names?

Answer:

If we implement multipole interface in the same class with conflict method name so we don't need to define all or in other words we can say if we have conflict methods in same class so we can't implement their body independently in the same class coz of same name and same signature so we have to use interface name before method name to remove this method confiscation let's see an example:

```
1.  interface testInterface1 {
2.      void Show();
3.  }
4.  interface testInterface2 {
5.      void Show();
6.  }
7.  class Abc: testInterface1,
8.  testInterface2 {
9.
10.     void testInterface1.Show() {
11.         Console.WriteLine("For testInterface1
    !!");
12.     }
```

```
13.     void testInterface2.Show() {
14.         Console.WriteLine("For testInterface2
    !!");
15.     }
16. }
```

Now see how to use those in a class:

```
1.  class Program {
2.      static void Main(string[] args) {
3.          testInterface1 obj1 = new Abc();
4.          testInterface1 obj2 = new Abc();
5.          obj1.Show();
6.          obj2.Show();
7.
8.          Console.ReadLine();
9.      }
10. }
```

Output:

23. What are the Arrays in C#.Net?

Answer:

Arrays are powerful data structures for solving many programming problems. You saw during the creation of variables of many types that they have one thing in common, they hold information about a single item, for instance an integer, float and string type and so on. So what is the solution if you need to manipulate sets of items? One solution would be to create a variable for each item in the set but again this leads to a different problem. How many variables do you need?

So in this situation Arrays provide mechanisms that solves problem posed by these questions. An array is a collection of related items, either value or reference type. In C# arrays are immutable such that the number of dimensions and size of the array are fixed.

Arrays   **Overview**

An array contains zero or more items called elements. An array is an unordered sequence of elements. All the elements in an array are of the same type (unlike fields in a class that can be of different types). The elements of an array accessed using an integer index that always starts from zero. C# supports single-dimensional (vectors), multidimensional and jagged arrays.

Elements are identified by indexes relative to the beginning of the arrays. An index is also commonly called indices or subscripts and are placed inside the indexing operator ([]). Access to array elements is by their index value that ranges from 0 to (length-1).

Array Properties

- The length cannot be changed once created.
- Elements are initialized to default values.
- Arrays are reference types and are instances of System.Array.
- Their number of dimensions or ranks can be determined by the Rank property.
- An array length can be determined by the GetLength() method or Length property.

24. What is the Constructor Chaining in C#?

Answer:

Constructor chaining is a way to connect two or more classes in a relationship as Inheritance, in Constructor Chaining every child class constructor is mapped to parent class Constructor implicitly by base keyword so when you create an instance of child class to it'll call parent's class Constructor without it inheritance is not possible.

Constructor chaining enables the calling of one constructor from another within the same class or between the base and derived classes. It allows the initialization logic defined in one constructor to be reused by other constructors, reducing code duplication and improving maintainability.

In C#, constructor chaining is achieved using this and base keywords. While the base keyword is used to call a constructor in the base class and this keyword is used to call another constructor in the same class.

25. What's the difference between the System.Array.CopyTo() and System.Array.Clone()?

Answer:

Clone:

Method creates a shallow copy of an array. A shallow copy of an Array copies only the elements of the Array, whether they are reference types or value types, but it does not copy the objects that the references refer to. The references in the new Array point to the same objects that the references in the original Array point to.

CopyTo:

The Copy static method of the Array class copies a section of an array to another array. The CopyTo method copies all the elements of an array to another one-dimension array. The code listed in Listing 9 copies contents of an integer array to an array of object types.

26. Can Multiple Catch Blocks executed in c#?

Answer:

we can use multiple Catches block with every try but when any Exceptions is throw by debugger so every catches match this exception type with their signature and catch the exception by any single catch block so that means we can use multiple catches blocks but only one can executed at once like:

```
1.  using System;
2.  class MyClient {
3.      public static void Main() {
4.          int x = 0;
5.          int div = 0;
6.          try {
7.              div = 100 / x;
8.              Console.WriteLine("Not executed l
    ine");
9.          } catch (DivideByZeroException de) {

10.             Console.WriteLine("DivideByZeroEx
    ception");
11.         } catch (Exception ee) {
12.             Console.WriteLine("Exception");
13.         } finally {
14.             Console.WriteLine("Finally Block"
    );
15.         }
16.         Console.WriteLine("Result is {0}", di
    v);
17.     }
18. }
```

27. What is Singleton Design Patterns and How to implement in C#?

Answer:

What is Singleton Design Pattern?

1. Ensures a class has only one instance and provides a global point of access to it.
2. A singleton is a class that only allows a single instance of itself to be created, and usually gives simple access to that instance.
3. Most commonly, singletons don't allow any parameters to be specified when creating the instance, since a second request of an instance with a different parameter could be problematic! (If the same instance should be accessed for all requests with the same parameter then the factory pattern is more appropriate.)
4. There are various ways to implement the Singleton Pattern in C#. The following are the common characteristics of a Singleton Pattern.

   • A single constructor, that is private and parameterless.
   •   The   class   is   sealed.
   • A static variable that holds a reference to the single   created   instance,   if   any.
   • A public static means of getting the reference to the single created instance, creating one if necessary.

This is the example how to write the code with Singleton:

```
1.  namespace Singleton {
2.      class Program {
```

```
3.          static void Main(string[] args) {
4.              Calculate.Instance.ValueOne = 10.
    5;
5.              Calculate.Instance.ValueTwo = 5.5
    ;
6.              Console.WriteLine("Addition : " +
    Calculate.Instance.Addition());
7.              Console.WriteLine("Subtraction :
    " + Calculate.Instance.Subtraction());
8.              Console.WriteLine("Multiplication
    : " + Calculate.Instance.Multiplication());

9.              Console.WriteLine("Division : " +
    Calculate.Instance.Division());
10.
11.             Console.WriteLine("\n------------
    ----------\n");
12.
13.             Calculate.Instance.ValueTwo = 10.
    5;
14.             Console.WriteLine("Addition : " +
    Calculate.Instance.Addition());
15.             Console.WriteLine("Subtraction :
    " + Calculate.Instance.Subtraction());
16.             Console.WriteLine("Multiplication
    : " + Calculate.Instance.Multiplication());

17.             Console.WriteLine("Division : " +
    Calculate.Instance.Division());
18.
19.             Console.ReadLine();
20.         }
21.     }
22.
23.     public sealed class Calculate {
24.         private Calculate() {}
25.         private static Calculate instance = n
    ull;
26.         public static Calculate Instance {
27.             get {
28.                 if (instance == null) {
29.                     instance = new Calculate(
    );
30.                 }
31.                 return instance;
32.             }
33.         }
34.
35.         public double ValueOne {
```

```
36.              get;
37.              set;
38.          }
39.          public double ValueTwo {
40.              get;
41.              set;
42.          }
43.
44.          public double Addition() {
45.              return ValueOne + ValueTwo;
46.          }
47.
48.          public double Subtraction() {
49.              return ValueOne - ValueTwo;
50.          }
51.
52.          public double Multiplication() {
53.              return ValueOne * ValueTwo;
54.          }
55.
56.          public double Division() {
57.              return ValueOne / ValueTwo;
58.          }
59.      }
60. }
```

28. Difference between Throw Exception and Throw Clause

Answer:

The basic difference is that the Throw exception overwrites the stack trace and this makes it hard to find the original code line number that has thrown the exception.

Throw basically retains the stack information and adds to the stack information in the exception that it is thrown.

Let us see what it means rather speaking so many words to better understand the differences. I am using a console application to easily test and see how the usage of the two differ in their functionality.

```
1.  using System;
2.  using System.Collections.Generic;
3.  using System.Linq;
4.  using System.Text;
5.
6.  namespace TestingThrowExceptions {
7.      class Program {
8.          public void ExceptionMethod() {
9.              throw new Exception("Original Exc
    eption occurred in ExceptionMethod");
10.
11.         }
12.
13.         static void Main(string[] args) {
14.             Program p = new Program();
15.             try {
16.                 p.ExceptionMethod();
17.             } catch (Exception ex) {
18.
19.                 throw ex;
20.             }
21.         }
22.     }
23. }
```

Now run the code by pressing the F5 key of the keyboard and see what happens. It returns an exception and look at the stack trace:

29. What are Indexer in C# .Net?

Answer:

Indexer allows classes to be used in more intuitive manner. C# introduces a new concept known as Indexers which are used for treating an object as an array. The indexers are usually known as smart arrays in C#. They are not essential part of object-oriented programming.

An indexer, also called an indexed property, is a class property that allows you to access a member variable of a class using the features of an array.

Defining an indexer allows you to create classes that act like virtual arrays. Instances of that class can be accessed using the [] array access operator.

Creating an Indexer

```
1.  < modifier > <
2.  return type > this[argument list] {
3.      get {
4.          // your get block code
5.      }
6.
7.      set {
8.          // your set block code
9.      }
10. }
```

In   the   above   code:

<modifier>

can be private, public, protected or internal.

<return   type>

can   be   any   valid   C#   types.

30. Difference between Equality Operator (==) and Equals() Method in C#

Answer:

Both the == Operator and the Equals() method are used to compare two value type data items or reference type data items. The Equality Operator (==) is the comparison operator and the Equals() method compares the contents of a string. The == Operator compares the reference identity while the Equals() method compares only contents. Let's see with some examples.

In this example we assigned a string variable to another variable. A string is a reference type and in the following example, a string variable is assigned to another string variable so they are referring to the same identity in the heap and both have the same content so you get True output for both the == Operator and the Equals() method.

```
1.  using System;
2.  namespace ComparisionExample {
3.      class Program {
4.          static void Main(string[] args) {
5.              string name = "sandeep";
6.              string myName = name;
7.              Console.WriteLine("== operator re
    sult is {0}", name == myName);
8.              Console.WriteLine("Equals method
    result is {0}", name.Equals(myName));
9.              Console.ReadKey();
10.         }
11.     }
12. }
```

31. Difference between is and as operator in C#

Answer:

"is" operator

In the C# language, we use the "is" operator to check the object type. If the two objects are of the same type, it returns true and false if not.

Let's understand the preceding from a small program.

We defined the following two classes:

```
1.  class Speaker {
2.      public string Name {
3.          get;
4.          set;
5.      }
6.  }
7.  class Author {
8.      public string Name {
9.          get;
10.         set;
11.     }
12. }
```

Now, let's try to check the preceding types as:

```
1.  var speaker = new Speaker { Name="Gaurav Kuma
    r Arora"};
```

We declared an object of Speaker as in the following:

```
1.  var isTrue = speaker is Speaker;
```

In the preceding, we are just checking the matching type. Yes, our speaker is an object of Speaker type.

```
1.  Console.WriteLine("speaker is of Speaker type
    :{0}", isTrue);
```

So, the results as true.

But, here we get false:

```
1.  var author = new Author { Name = "Gaurav Kuma
    r Arora" };
2.  var isTrue = speaker is Author;
3.  Console.WriteLine("speaker is of Author type:
    {0}", isTrue);
```

Because our our speaker is not an object of Author type.

"as" operator:

The "as" operator behaves similar to the "is" operator. The only difference is it returns the object if both are compatible to that type else it returns null.

Let's understand the preceding with a small snippet as in the following:

```
1.  public static string GetAuthorName(dynamic ob
    j)
2.  {
3.  Author authorObj = obj as Author;
4.  return (authorObj != null) ? authorObj.Name :
    string.Empty;
5.  }
```

We have a method that accepts dynamic objects and returns the object name property if the object is of the Author type.

Here, we declared two objects:

```
1.  var speaker = new Speaker { Name="Gaurav Kuma
    r Arora"};
2.  var author = new Author { Name = "Gaurav Kuma
    r Arora" };
```

The following returns the "Name" property:

```
1.  var authorName = GetAuthorName(author);
2.  Console.WriteLine("Author name is:{0}", autho
    rName);
```

It returns an empty string:

```
1.  authorName = GetAuthorName(speaker);
2.  Console.WriteLine("Author name is:{0}", autho
    rName);
```

32. How to use Nullable<> Types in .Net?

Answer:

A nullable Type is a data type is that contain the defined data type or the value of null.

You should note here that here variable datatype has been given and then only it can be used.

This nullable type concept is not comaptible with "var".

I will explain this with syntax in next section.

Declaration:

Any DataType can be declared nullable type with the help of operator "?".

Example of the syntax is as Follows :-

```
1.  int? i = null;
```

As discussed in previous section "var" is not compatible with this Nullable Type.

So we will have Compile Time error if we are declaring something like: -

```
1.  var? i = null;
```

though following syntax is completely fine :-

```
1.  var i = 4;
```

33. Different Ways of Method can be overloaded

Answer:

Method overloading is a way to achieve compile time Polymorphism where we can use a method with the same name but different signature, Method overloading is done at compile time and we have multiple way to do that but in all way method name should be same.

- Number of parameter can be different.
- Types of parameter can be different.
- Order of parameters can be different.

Example:

```
1.  using System;
2.  using System.Collections.Generic;
3.  using System.Linq;
4.  using System.Text;
5.
6.  namespace Hello_Word {
7.      class overloding {
8.          public static void Main() {
9.              Console.WriteLine(volume(10));
10.             Console.WriteLine(volume(2.5F, 8)
    );
11.             Console.WriteLine(volume(100L, 75
    , 15));
12.             Console.ReadLine();
13.         }
14.
15.         static int volume(int x) {
16.             return (x * x * x);
17.         }
18.
19.         static double volume(float r, int h)
    {
20.             return (3.14 * r * r * h);
21.         }
22.
23.         static long volume(long l, int b, int
    h) {
24.             return (l * b * h);
25.         }
26.     }
27. }
```

Note:

If we have a method that have two parameter object type and have a same name method with two integer parameter so when we call that method with int value so it'll call that method have integer parameter instead of object type parameters method.

34. What is an Object Pool in .Net?

Answer:

Object Pooling is something that tries to keep a pool of objects in memory to be re-used later and hence it will reduce the load of object creation to a great extent. This article will try to explain this in detail. The example is for an Employee object, but you can make it general by using Object base class.

What does it mean?

Object Pool is nothing but a container of objects that are ready for use. Whenever there is a request for a new object, the pool manager will take the request and it will be served by allocating an object from the pool.

How it works?

We are going to use Factory pattern for this purpose. We will have a factory method, which will take care about the creation of objects. Whenever there is a request for a new object, the factory method will look into the object pool (we use Queue object). If there is any object available within the allowed limit, it will return the object (value object), otherwise a new object will be created and give you back.

35. What are generics in c#.net?

Answer:

Generics allow you to delay the specification of the data type of programming elements in a class or a method, until it is actually used in the program. In other words, generics allow you to write a class or method that can work with any data type.

You write the specifications for the class or the method, with substitute parameters for data types. When the compiler encounters a constructor for the class or a function call for the method, it generates code to handle the specific data type.

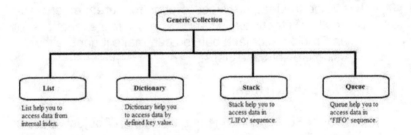

Generic classes and methods combine reusability, type safety and efficiency in a way that their non-generic counterparts cannot. Generics are most frequently used with collections and the methods that operate on them. Version 2.0 of the .NET Framework class library provides a new namespace, System.Collections.Generic, that contains several new generic-based collection classes. It is recommended that all applications that target the .NET Framework 2.0 and later use the new generic collection classes instead of the older non-generic counterparts such as ArrayList.

Features of Generics

Generics is a technique that enriches your programs in the following ways:

- It helps you to maximize code reuse, type safety and performance.
- You can create generic collection classes. The .NET Framework class library contains several new generic collection classes in the System.Collections.Generic namespace. You may use these generic collection classes instead of the collection classes in the System.Collections namespace.
- You can create your own generic interfaces, classes, methods, events and delegates.
- You may create generic classes constrained to enable access to methods on specific data types.
- You may get information on the types used in a generic data type at run-time using reflection.

36. Describe the accessibility modifiers in c#

Answer:

Access modifiers are keywords used to specify the declared accessibility of a member or a type.

Why to use access modifiers?

Access modifiers are an integral part of object-oriented programming. They support the concept of encapsulation, which promotes the idea of hiding functionality. Access modifiers allow you to define who does or doesn't have access to certain features.
In C# there are 5 different types of Access Modifiers.

Modifier	Description
public	There are no restrictions on accessing public members.
private	Access is limited to within the class definition. This is the default access modifier type if none is formally specified
protected	Access is limited to within the class definition and any class that inherits from the class
internal	Access is limited exclusively to classes defined within the current project assembly
protected internal	Access is limited to the current assembly and

37. What is Virtual Method in C#?

Answer:

A virtual method is a method that can be redefined in derived classes. A virtual method has an implementation in a base class as well as derived the class. It is used when a method's basic functionality is the same but sometimes more functionality is needed in the derived class. A virtual method is created in the base class that can be overridden in the derived class. We create a virtual method in the base class using the virtual keyword and that method is overridden in the derived class using the override keyword.

When a method is declared as a virtual method in a base class then that method can be defined in a base class and it is optional for the derived class to override that method. The overriding method also provides more than one form for a method. Hence it is also an example for polymorphism.

When a method is declared as a virtual method in a base class and that method has the same definition in a derived class then there is no need to override it in the derived class. But when a virtual method has a different definition in the base class and the derived class then there is a need to override it in the derived class.

When a virtual method is invoked, the run-time type of the object is checked for an overriding member. The overriding member in the most derived class is called, which might be the original member, if no derived class has overridden the member.

Virtual Method

1. By default, methods are non-virtual. We can't override a non-virtual method.
2. We can't use the virtual modifier with the static, abstract, private or override modifiers.

38. What are the Difference between Array and ArrayList in C#.Net?

Answer:

Difference   between   Array   and   ArrayList

Array	ArrayList
Array uses the Vector array to store the elements	ArrayList uses the Linked List to store the elements.
Size of the Array must be defined until redeem used(vb)	No need to specify the storage size.
Array is a specific data type storage	ArrayList can be stored everything as object.
No need to do the type casting	Every time type casting has to do.
It will not lead to Runtime exception	It leads to the Run time error exception.
Element cannot be inserted or deleted in between.	Elements can be inserted and deleted.
There is no built in members to do ascending or descending.	ArrayList has many methods to do operation like Sort, Insert, Remove, Binary Search, etc..,

What is an Array

An array is a collection of elements of the same type, stored in contiguous memory locations. Arrays can be declared and used in many ways, including specifying the type of elements, the number of elements, and their names.

Advantages of Array

The following are some of the advantages of using Arrays in C#:

- Speed: A contiguous memory location makes Arrays faster than ArrayLists when it comes to accessing and manipulating elements.
- Memory Efficiency: Arrays are more memory-efficient than ArrayLists since metadata and other information are not stored in additional memory.
- Type Safety: It is useful for preventing type mismatches and other errors to use arrays because they are type-safe.

- Simplicity: Basic data manipulation tasks can be accomplished with arrays because they are easy to use and understand.
- Built-in Support: A variety of built-in functions and methods can be used with arrays in C# and other programming languages.
- Less overhead then ArrayList: Because arraylists have more functionality, they are more complex than arrays.

What is Arraylist

An ArrayList is a dynamic array that can hold elements of different data types in C#. It is part of System. Collections, and allows for resizing as elements are added or removed. Besides providing many useful methods for working with lists of items, it also has Add, Remove, and IndexOf methods. However, it is less efficient than a generic List<T> for strongly-typed lists, and should only be used when the data type of the elements is not known at compile-time.

Advantages of Arraylist

There are several advantages of using ArrayList in C#:

- Dynamic Size: ArrayLists automatically resize themselves as elements are added or removed, so you don't need to specify the size when you create them.
- Type Safety: In contrast to an array, which can only store elements of a specific type, an arrayList can store elements of any type.
- Built-in Methods: In addition to adding, removing, and searching for elements, ArrayList provides several built-in methods.
- Sorting and Searching: ArrayLists provide methods for sorting and searching their elements, making them more powerful than arrays.

- Thread Safety: Multiple threads can access an ArrayList without causing errors since ArrayLists are thread-safe.
- Memory Efficient: When the number of elements in a collection changes frequently, an arrayList is more memory-efficient than an array.

39. What you understand by Value types and Reference types in C#.Net?

Answer:

In C# data types can be of two types: Value Types and Reference Types. Value type variables contain their object (or data) directly. If we copy one value type variable to another then we are actually making a copy of the object for the second variable. Both of them will independently operate on their values, Value Type member will located into Stack and reference member will located in Heap always.

Let consider each case briefly.

1. **Pure**   **Value**   **Type**

   Here I used a structure as a value type. It has an integer member. I created two instances of this structure. Afterwards I assigned second instance to the first one. Then I changed the state of second instance, but it hasn't effect the first one, as whole items are value type and assignments on those types will copy only values not references i.e. in a Value Type assignment, all instances have its own local copy of members.

2. **Pure**   **Reference**   **Type**

I created a class and added a "DataTable" as a Reference Type member for this class. Then I performed the assignments just like below. But the difference is that on changing the state of second instance, the state of first instance will automatically alter. So in a Reference Type assignment both Value and Reference will be assigned i.e. all instances will point to the single object.

3. **Value Type With Reference Type**

This case and the last case to come are more interesting. I used a structure in this particular scenario also. But this time it includes a Reference Type(A Custom Class Object) Member besides a Value Type (An Integer) Member. When you performing the assignments, it seems like a swallow copy, as Value Type member of first instance won't effected, but the Reference Type member will alter according to the second instance. So in this particular scenario, assignment of Reference Type member produced a reference to a single object and assignment of Value Type member produced a local copy of that member.

4. **Reference Type With Value Type**

Contrary to the above case, in this scenario, both Reference & Value Types will be effected. I.e. a Value Type member in a Reference Type will be shared among its instances.

40. What is Serialization?

Answer:

Serialization means saving the state of your object to secondary memory, such as a file.

Suppose you have a business layer where you have many classes to perform your business data.

Now suppose you want to test whether your business classes give the correct data out without verifying the result from the UI or from a database. Because it will take some time to process.

SO what you will you do my friend?

Here comes Serialization. You will serialize all your necessary business classes and save them into a text or XML file.

on your hard disk. So you can easily test your desired result by comparing your serialized saved data with.

your desired output data. You can say it is a little bit of autonomic unit testing performed by the developer.

There are three types of serialization:

1. Binary serialization (Save your object data into binary format).
2. Soap Serialization (Save your object data into binary format; mainly used in network related communication).
3. XmlSerialization (Save your object data into an XML file).

41. What is the use of Using statement in C#?

Answer:

The .Net Framework provides resource management for managed objects through the garbage collector - You do not have to explicitly allocate and release memory for managed objects. Clean-up operations for any unmanaged resources should performed in the destructor in C#. To allow the programmer to explicitly perform these clean-up activities, objects can provide a Dispose method that can be invoked when the object is no longer needed. The using statement in C# defines a boundary for the object outside of which, the object is automatically destroyed. The using statement is excited when the end of the "using" statement block or the execution exits the "using" statement block indirectly, for example - an exception is thrown. The "using" statement allows you to specify multiple resources in a single statement. The object could also be created outside the "using" statement. The objects specified within the using block must implement the IDisposable interface. The framework invokes the Dispose method of objects specified within the "using" statement when the block is exited.

42. What is jagged array in C#.Net?

Answer:

A jagged array is an array whose elements are arrays. The elements of a jagged array can be of different dimensions and sizes. A jagged array is sometimes called an "array of arrays."

A special type of array is introduced in C#. A Jagged Array is an array of an array in which the length of each array index can differ.

Example:

```
1.  int[][] jagArray = new int[5][];
```

In the above declaration the rows are fixed in size. But columns are not specified as they can vary.

Declaring and initializing jagged array.

```
1.  int[][] jaggedArray = new int[5][];
2.
3.  jaggedArray[0] = new int[3];
4.  jaggedArray[1] = new int[5];
5.  jaggedArray[2] = new int[2];
6.  jaggedArray[3] = new int[8];
7.  jaggedArray[4] = new int[10];
8.  jaggedArray[0] = new int[] { 3, 5, 7, };
9.  jaggedArray[1] = new int[] { 1, 0, 2, 4, 6 };

10. jaggedArray[2] = new int[] { 1, 6 };
11. jaggedArray[3] = new int[] { 1, 0, 2, 4, 6, 4
    5, 67, 78 };
12. jaggedArray[4] = new int[] { 1, 0, 2, 4, 6, 3
    4, 54, 67, 87, 78 };
```

43. What is Multithreading with .NET?

Answer:

The real usage of a thread is not about a single sequential thread, but rather using multiple threads in a single program. Multiple threads running at the same time and performing various tasks is referred as Multithreading. A thread is considered to be a lightweight process because it runs within the context of a program and takes advantage of resources allocated for that program.

A single-threaded process contains only one thread while a multithreaded process contains more than one thread for execution.

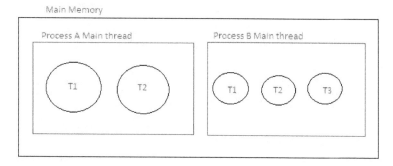

System.Threading **Namespace**

Like many other features, in .NET, System.Threading is the namespace that provides various types to help in construction of multithreaded applications.

Type	Description
Thread	It represents a thread that executes within the CLR. Using this, we can produce additional threads in an application domain.
Mutex	It is used for synchronization between application domains.
Monitor	It implements synchronization of objects using Locks and Wait.
Smaphore	It allows limiting the number of threads that can access a resource concurrently.
Interlock	It provides atomic operations for variables that are shared by multiple threads.
ThreadPool	It allows you to interact with the CLR maintained thread pool.
ThreadPriority	This represents the priority level such as High, Normal, and Low.

44. Explain Anonymous type in C#?

Answer:

Anonymous types allow us to create new type without defining them. This is way to defining read only properties into a single object without having to define type explicitly. Here Type is generating by the compiler and it is accessible only for the current block of code. The type of properties is also inferred by the compiler.

We can create anonymous types by using "new" keyword together with the object initializer.

Example

```
1.  var anonymousData = new
2.  {
3.      ForeName = "Jignesh",
4.      SurName = "Trivedi"
5.  };
6.  Console.WriteLine("First Name : " + anonymous
    Data.ForeName);
```

Anonymous Types with LINQ Example

Anonymous types are also used with the "Select" clause of LINQ query expression to return subset of properties.

Example

If Any object collection having properties called FirstName , LastName, DOB etc. and you want only FirstName and LastName after the Querying the data then.

```
1.  class MyData {
2.      public string FirstName {
3.          get;
4.          set;
5.      }
6.      public string LastName {
7.          get;
8.          set;
9.      }
10.     public DateTime DOB {
11.         get;
12.         set;
13.     }
14.     public string MiddleName {
15.         get;
16.         set;
```

```
17.     }
18. }
19. static void Main(string[] args) {
20.     // Create Dummy Data to fill Collection.

21.     List < MyData > data = new List < MyData
    > ();
22.     data.Add(new MyData {
23.         FirstName = "Jignesh", LastName = "Tr
    ivedi", MiddleName = "G", DOB = new DateTime(
    1990, 12, 30)
24.     });
25.     data.Add(new MyData {
26.         FirstName = "Tejas", LastName = "Triv
    edi", MiddleName = "G", DOB = new DateTime(19
    95, 11, 6)
27.     });
28.     data.Add(new MyData {
29.         FirstName = "Rakesh", LastName = "Tri
    vedi", MiddleName = "G", DOB = new DateTime(1
    993, 10, 8)
30.     });
31.     data.Add(new MyData {
32.         FirstName = "Amit", LastName = "Vyas"
    , MiddleName = "P", DOB = newDateTime(1983, 6
    , 15)
33.     });
34.     data.Add(new MyData {
35.         FirstName = "Yash", LastName = "Pandi
    ya", MiddleName = "K", DOB = newDateTime(1988
    , 7, 20)
36.     });
37. }
38. var anonymousData = from pl in data
39. select new {
40.     pl.FirstName, pl.LastName
41. };
42. foreach(var m in anonymousData) {
43.     Console.WriteLine("Name : " + m.FirstName
    + " " + m.LastName);
44. }
45. }
```

45. Explain Hashtable in C#?

Answer:

A Hashtable is a collection that stores (Keys, Values) pairs. Here, the Keys are used to find the storage location and is immutable and cannot have duplicate entries in the Hashtable. The .Net Framework has provided a Hash Table class that contains all the functionality required to implement a hash table without any additional development. The hash table is a general-purpose dictionary collection. Each item within the collection is a DictionaryEntry object with two properties: a key object and a value object. These are known as Key/Value. When items are added to a hash table, a hash code is generated automatically. This code is hidden from the developer. All access to the table's values is achieved using the key object for identification. As the items in the collection are sorted according to the hidden hash code, the items should be considered to be randomly ordered.

The   Hashtable   Collection

The Base Class libraries offers a Hashtable Class that is defined in the System.Collections namespace, so you don't have to code your own hash tables. It processes each key of the hash that you add every time and then uses the hash code to look up the element very quickly. The capacity of a hash table is the number of elements the hash table can hold. As elements are added to a hash table, the capacity is automatically increased as required through reallocation. It is an older .Net Framework type.

Declaring   a   Hashtable

The Hashtable class is generally found in the namespace called System.Collections. So to execute any of the examples, we have to add using System.Collections; to the source code. The declaration for the Hashtable is:

```
1.  Hashtable HT = new Hashtable ();
```

46. What is LINQ in C#?

Answer:

LINQ stands for Language Integrated Query. LINQ is a data querying methodology which provides querying capabilities to .NET languages with a syntax similar to a SQL   query

LINQ has a great power of querying on any source of data. The data source could be collections of objects, database or XML files. We can easily retrieve data from any object that implements the IEnumerable<T> interface.

Advantages of LINQ

1. LINQ offers an object-based, language-integrated way to query over data no matter where that data came from. So through LINQ we can query database, XML as well as collections.

2. Compile   time   syntax   checking.

3. It allows you to query collections like arrays, enumerable classes etc in the native language of your application, like VB or C# in much the same way as you would query a database using SQL.

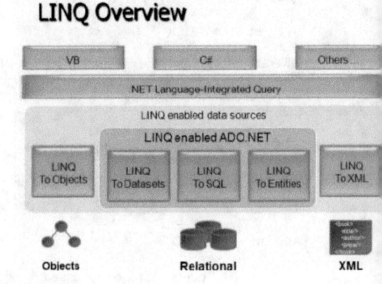

47. What is File Handling in C#.Net?

Answer:

The System.IO namespace provides four classes that allow you to manipulate individual files, as well as interact with a machine directory structure. The Directory and File directly extends System.Object and supports the creation, copying, moving and deletion of files using various static methods. They only contain static methods and are never instantiated. The FileInfo and DirecotryInfo types are derived from the abstract class FileSystemInfo type and they are typically, employed for obtaining the full details of a file or directory because their members tend to return strongly typed objects. They implement roughly the same public methods as a Directory and a File but they are stateful and the members of these classes are not static.

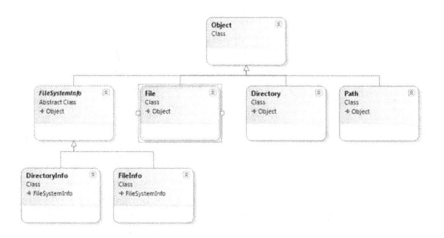

48. What is Reflection in C#.Net?

Answer:

Reflection typically is the process of runtime type discovery to inspect metadata, CIL code, late binding and self-generating code. At run time by using reflection, we can access the same "type" information as displayed by the ildasm utility at design time. The reflection is analogous to reverse engineering in which we can break an existing *.exe or *.dll assembly to explore defined significant contents information, including methods, fields, events and properties.

You can dynamically discover the set of interfaces supported by a given type using the System.Reflection namespace. This namespace contains numerous related types as follows:

Types	Description
Assembly	This static class allows you to load, investigate and manipulate an assembly.
AssemblyName	Allows to exploration of abundant details behind an assembly.
EventInfo	Information about a given event.
PropertyInfo	Holds information of a specified property.
MethodInfo	Contains information about a specified method.

Reflection typically is used to dump out the loaded assemblies list, their reference to inspect methods, properties etcetera. Reflection is also used in the external disassembling tools such Reflector, Fxcop and NUnit because .NET tools don't need to parse the source code similar   to   C++.

Metadata   Investigation

The following program depicts the process of reflection by creating a console based application. This program will display the details of the fields, methods, properties and interfaces for any type within the mscorlib.dll assembly. Before proceeeding, it is mandatory to import "System.Reflection".

Here, we are defining a number of static methods in the program class to enumerate fields, methods and interfaces in the specified type. The static method takes a single "System.Type" parameter and returns void.

```
1.  static void FieldInvestigation(Type t) {
2.      Console.WriteLine("*********Fields*******
    **");
3.      FieldInfo[] fld = t.GetFields();
4.      foreach(FieldInfo f in fld) {
5.          Console.WriteLine("--
    >{0}", f.Name);
6.      }
7.  }
8.
9.  static void MethodInvestigation(Type t) {
10.     Console.WriteLine("*********Methods******
    ***");
11.     MethodInfo[] mth = t.GetMethods();
12.     foreach(MethodInfo m in mth) {
13.         Console.WriteLine("--
    >{0}", m.Name);
14.     }
15. }
```

49. Types of Constructors in C#?

Whenever an instance of a class or a struct is created, its constructor is called. A class or struct may have multiple constructors that take different arguments. Constructors enable the programmer to set default values, limit instantiation, and write code that is flexible and easy to read. A Constructor is a special method of the class that is automatically invoked when an instance of the class is created is called a constructor. The main use of constructors is to initialize the private fields of the class while creating an instance for the class. When you have not created a constructor in the class, the compiler will automatically create a default constructor of the class. The default constructor initializes all numeric fields in the class to zero and all string and object fields to null.

There are several actions that are part of initializing a new instance. Those actions take place in the following order:

- Instance fields are set to 0. This is typically done by the runtime.
- Field initializers run. The field initializers in the most derived type run.
- Base type field initializers run. Field initializers starting with the direct base through each base type to System.Object.
- Base instance constructors run. Any instance constructors, starting with Object.Object through each base class to the direct base class.
- The instance constructor runs. The instance constructor for the type runs.
- Object initializers run. If the expression includes any object initializers, those run after the instance constructor runs. Object initializers run in the textual order.

In C#, constructors can be divided into 5 types

1. Default Constructor
2. Parameterized Constructor

3. Copy Constructor
4. Static Constructor
5. Private Constructor

Default Constructor in C#

A constructor without any parameters is called a default constructor; in other words, this type of constructor does not take parameters. The drawback of a default constructor is that every instance of the class will be initialized to the same values and it is not possible to initialize each instance of the class with different values. The default constructor initializes:

- All numeric fields in the class to zero.
- All string and object fields to null.

```
class addition
{
    int a, b;
    public addition()    //default contructor
    {
        a = 100;
        b = 175;
    }

    public static void Main()
    {
        addition obj = new addition(); //an object is
        Console.WriteLine(obj.a);
        Console.WriteLine(obj.b);
        Console.Read();
    }
}
```

Parameterized Constructor in C#

A constructor with at least one parameter is called a parameterized constructor. The advantage of a parameterized constructor is that you can initialize each instance of the class with a different value.

```
class paraconstrctor
{
    public  int a, b;
    public paraconstrctor(int x, int y)
    {
        a = x;
        b = y;
    }
}
```

Copy Constructor in C#

The constructor which creates an object by copying variables from another object is called a copy constructor. The purpose of a copy constructor is to initialize a new instance to the values of an existing instance.

```
public employee(employee emp)
{
    name=emp.name;
    age=emp.age;
}
```

Static Constructor in C#

When a constructor is created using a static keyword, it will be invoked only once for all of the instances of the class and it is invoked during the creation of the first instance of the class or the first reference to a static member in the class. A static constructor is used to initialize static fields of the class and to write the code that needs to be executed only once.
Some key points of a static constructor are:

- A static constructor does not take access modifiers or have parameters.
- A static constructor is called automatically to initialize the class before the first instance is created or any static members are referenced.
- A static constructor cannot be called directly.
- The user has no control over when the static constructor is executed in the program.
- A typical use of static constructors is when the class is using a log file and the constructor is used to write entries to this file.

```
class employee
{
    // Static constructor
    static employee(){}
}
```

50. What is the difference between a class having private constructor and a sealed class having private constructor?

A sealed class can be instantiated but a class with a private constructor can not. They both don't allow inheritance, but that's not the objective of a private constructor.

The reason you use a private constructor is to stop instantiation. This is often used in static factory methods, where you must call MyClass::Create(...) to create an instance.

51. What is SOLID principles?

In Object Oriented Programming (OOP), SOLID is an acronym, introduced by Michael Feathers, for five design principles used to make software design more

understandable, flexible, and maintainable. SOLID stands for the following:
- S = Single Responsibility Principle
- O = Open Closed Principle
- L = Liskov Substitution Principle
- I = Interface Segregation Principle
- D = Dependency Inversion Principle

S: Single-responsibility principle
"A class should only have a single responsibility, that is, only changes to one part of the software's specification should be able to affect the specification of the class."

Each should take the job for a single functionality of the program. The class should comprise only methods and variables relevant to its functionality. Classes can function together to accomplish larger complicated tasks, but every class must execute a function from the beginning to the end before it sends the output to another class. Martin described this by stating "a class should have only one reason to change". Here, the "reason" is that we wish to alter the single functionality this class pursues. If we do not choose this single functionality to vary, we will never alter this class, as all components of the class should relate to that behaviour.

O: Open/Closed Principle (OCP)
This is the second principle of Solid Principles, which is described as follows:
"A software class or module should be open for extension but closed for modification."

If we have jotted a class, then it has to be flexible enough that we should not modify it (closed for modification) until bugs are there, but a new feature can be incorporated (open for extension) by implementing a new code without changing its existing code. This principle highlights that it should be plausible to expand functionality in classes without the need to alter the existing code in the classes. i.e. it should be feasible to expand the behaviour of the software without changing its core existing implementation.

L: Liskov Substitution Principle
"Objects in a program should be replaceable with instances of their subtypes without altering the correctness of that program."

The Liskov Substitution Principle (LSP) states, "you should be able to use any derived class instead of a parent class and have it behave in the same manner without modification.". It ensures that a derived class does not affect the behavior of the parent class; in other words, a derived class must be substitutable for its base class.
This principle is just an extension of the Open Closed Principle, and we must ensure that newly derived classes extend the base classes without changing their behavior.
I will explain this with a real-world example that violates LSP.
A father is a doctor, whereas his son wants to become a cricketer. So here, the son can't replace his father even though they belong to the same family hierarchy.

I: Interface Segregation Principle (ISP)
The Interface Segregation Principle states *"that clients should not be forced to implement interfaces they don't use. Instead of one fat interface, many small interfaces are preferred based on groups of methods, each serving one submodule."*

We can define it in another way. An interface should be more closely related to the code that uses it than the code that implements it. So the methods on the interface are defined by which methods the client code needs rather than which methods the class implements. So clients should not be forced to depend upon interfaces they don't use.
Like classes, each interface should have a specific purpose/responsibility (refer to SRP). You shouldn't be forced to implement an interface when your object doesn't share that purpose. The larger the interface, the

more likely it includes methods not all implementers can use. That's the essence of the Interface Segregation Principle. Let's start with an example that breaks the ISP. Suppose we need to build a system for an IT firm that contains roles like TeamLead and Programmer where TeamLead divides a huge task into smaller tasks and assigns them to his/her programmers or can directly work on them.

D: Dependency Inversion Principle

The Dependency Inversion Principle (DIP) states that *"high-level modules/classes should not depend on low-level modules/classes. First, both should depend upon abstractions. Secondly, abstractions should not rely upon details. Finally, details should depend upon abstractions."*

High-level modules/classes implement business rules or logic in a system (application). Low-level modules/classes deal with more detailed operations; in other words, they may write information to databases or pass messages to the operating system or services.
A high-level module/class that depends on low-level modules/classes or some other class and knows a lot about the other classes it interacts with is said to be tightly coupled. When a class knows explicitly about the design and implementation of another class, it raises the risk that changes to one class will break the other. So we must keep these high-level and low-level modules/classes loosely coupled as much as possible. To do that, we need to make both of them dependent on abstractions instead of knowing each other.

52. Explain Garbage Collector?

Garbage collection is a memory management technique used in the .NET Framework and many other programming languages. In C#, the garbage collector is responsible for managing memory and automatically freeing up memory that is no longer being used by the application.

The garbage collector works by periodically scanning the application's memory to determine which objects are still being used and which are no longer needed. Objects that are no longer being used are marked for garbage collection, and their memory is freed up automatically by the garbage collector.

Some of the key features of the garbage collector in C# include:

2   Automatic memory management: With the garbage collector, developers don't need to worry about manually allocating or freeing up memory. The garbage collector takes care of memory management automatically, which can help reduce the risk of memory leaks and other issues.

3   Low impact on application performance: The garbage collector runs in the background and typically has a low impact on application performance. However, in some cases, garbage collection can cause brief pauses or slowdowns in the application, particularly when large amounts of memory need to be freed up at once.

4   Generation-based collection: The garbage collector in C# uses a generation-based approach to memory management. Objects are initially allocated in a "young" generation and are moved to an "old" generation if they survive multiple garbage collection cycles. This approach helps reduce the amount of time required for garbage collection, as most objects are collected in the young generation.

5   Finalization: The garbage collector also provides support for finalization, which is a process that allows objects to perform cleanup tasks before they are destroyed. Objects with finalizers are moved to a separate finalization queue, which is processed by the garbage collector after all other objects have been collected.

There are mainly 3 phases in garbage collection. Details about these are given as follows:

Phase in Garbage Collection

Marking Phase
(List of live objects created)

Relocating Phase
(References for list of live ojects updated)

Compacting Phase
(Dead objects released & live objects compacted & moved)

1. **Marking Phase**: A list of all the live objects is created during the marking phase. This is done by following the references from all the root objects. All of the objects that are not on the list of live objects are potentially deleted from the heap memory.
2. **Relocating Phase**: The references of all the objects that were on the list of all the live objects are updated in the relocating phase so that they point to the new location where the objects will be relocated to in the compacting phase.
3. **Compacting Phase**: The heap gets compacted in the compacting phase as the space occupied by the dead objects is released and the live objects remaining are moved. All the live objects that remain after the garbage collection are moved towards the older end of the heap memory in their original order.

53. Explain CLR?

The Common Language Runtime (CLR) is a component of the Microsoft .NET Framework that manages the execution of .NET applications. It is responsible for loading and executing the code written in various .NET programming languages

- Suppose you have written a C# program and save it in a file which is known as the Source Code.
- Language specific compiler compiles the source code into the MSIL(Microsoft Intermediate Language) which is also known as the CIL(Common Intermediate Language) or IL(Intermediate Language) along with its metadata. Metadata includes all the types, actual implementation of each function of the program. MSIL is machine-independent code.
- Now CLR comes into existence. CLR provides the services and runtime environment to the MSIL code. Internally CLR includes the JIT(Just-In-Time) compiler which converts the MSIL code to machine code which further executed by CPU. CLR also uses the .NET Framework class libraries. Metadata provides information about the programming language, environment, version, and class libraries to the CLR by which CLR handles the MSIL code. As CLR is common so it allows an instance of a class that written in a different language to call a method of the class which written in another language.